Are You Ready To Serve?

Don Terry

Are You Ready To Serve? by Don Terry

Published in the United States. First edition.

Cover art by Brad Singleton

ISBN: 0615693911
ISBN-13: 978-0615693910

DEDICATION

This book is dedicated to all who serve God by working as either paid, or volunteer church staff. I also dedicate this book to my children, Silas and Logan, who I pray will grow to love and serve God's church.

CONTENTS

Introduction

The purpose of this book is to help people, who want to serve in their church, consider their hearts, motives, and abilities before entering church service. In addition, I offer some advice from over thirty years of church service.

I want to encourage you in your decision to serve, but I want to **be real** and help **prepare** you for what lies ahead. Each church has its own personality, challenges, blessings and curses.

Be ready to experience a little bit

of all of those.

As Christians, **we are called** to do more than sit back and receive. We are called to **serve**. The consumer mindset of "feed me" and "entertain me" is not an option. If you are reading this, you are at least considering doing more. The least you can do is **prepare yourself mentally and spiritually for the task ahead**. That is what I hope to help you accomplish. Be sure to ask your pastor and other Christian leaders in your church for advice along the way. Most of all, **don't forget to pray and seek answers in God's Word daily.**

Blessings to you as you serve God by serving His people.

Don, a fellow servant

1 ARE YOU SURE?

You are likely reading this because you are thinking about serving in your church. My first question is, "Are you sure?" I know you are wondering why I would ask that question. Maybe you think I've been jaded by bad experiences. Or, I have a bad attitude. After all, how can anyone doubt whether or not to serve at church?

I have had plenty of bad experiences both as a leader and as a follower. But, I'm not going to talk about those here. I ask my question in all sincerity. You, who want to serve in any capacity at your church, should **consider your motives** and have a certain level of **maturity**.

If you enter into church service either spiritually, or mentally unprepared, your experience could be most unpleasant. This book will give you some points of consideration in preparation of your service.

You are about to enter the world of church leadership. There's no reason to go as a lamb to the slaughter.

Matthew 10:16 says, "Behold, I send you out as sheep in the midst of wolves. Therefore be wise as serpents and harmless as doves."

Some of us have not had the best experiences with church leaders or parishioners.

Yet, we still serve. Why?

I can't speak for everyone's motives. I just know that I love serving in my local church because I know great things can happen there. I was introduced to relationship with God through Jesus Christ in church. I learned to worship God at church. I also learned to study His Word, and to live my life for Him.

I serve because I want to contribute to those experiences for others.

Wouldn't anyone want to be a part of an experience that **helps other people learn about and get closer to God**? Of course they would! But, there are some truths you need to consider and some soul searching to do if you want to succeed in your service to God and His people.

There are a lot of books about church service and much I could say. But I have written about the seven be-attitudes of church service.

Be a Servant

Be Patient

Be Strong

Be Flexible

Be Prepared

Be Real

Be Loving

2 BE A SERVANT

At some point in your service to the church, you will feel as though you are *taken for granted.* You will feel *taken advantage of, overlooked, overworked and underpaid;* if you are paid at all.

Whatever you do, if you are paid, **do not try to calculate what you really make hourly**.

It will depress you!

Another important point is if you are a servant, then **you should not expect to be served.** To be fair, some are treated quite well and some make a decent wage. But, if you are at it long enough, familiarity will creep in. Either you will become too familiar with your work; those you serve will become too familiar with you, or both.

It is human nature, **we get used to things**. The things of God can become common place. The joy and excitement you had when you started **will wear off**. People will get used to getting what you offer.

At some point, your fans **will stop telling** you what a wonderful singer you are. The congregation **will stop bragging** about your preaching or teaching.

They aren't likely to mention how beautiful the bulletins are, or how clean the bathrooms are.

But **they will let you know when they don't agree with you**, when they think something **should be done differently,** or when **something is wrong**.

Jesus said in Mark 9:35, "If anyone desires to be first, he shall be **last of all and servant of all.**"

Slaves have no rights or glory.

Servants and slaves have no impressive titles or business cards. They don't necessarily get noticed. So, if you're serving to try to get noticed, or to impress someone, **stop right now!**

You're not doing anyone any favors and you may actually do yourself, the church and those you are "serving" harm.

My friend Josh Brewer says, "If serving doesn't cost you something, the only one you're serving is yourself."

Look to Jesus as the model. With all power at His command and the God of creation as His Father, He washed the disciple's feet. (John 13:1-17)

This is our example:

Power and authority
in service to people
under the submission of God.

3 BE PATIENT

You will be criticized and you will be offended. People can be mean. Just because they are in church, doesn't mean they'll be any different. So you must have you have a thick skin.

Can you take criticism?

How do you react when your beliefs, policies and procedures are challenged? How do you feel when people don't like you, or what you represent?

If you are a leader, like it or not you will find out the answers to all of these questions. It's generally understood that religion and politics are the two main topics one does not bring up in conversation, unless one wants to cause trouble.

Just because you are in church, does not necessarily mean the topic of religion won't cause some problems.

People hold tight to their beliefs.

They invest in them and become **comfortable in their beliefs**. They may have learned what they believe from their parents, or grandparents.

If you are a teacher, or pastor, one day you will say something that challenges someone else's long-held beliefs.

You will say, or do something to offend people.

Here's where you have the opportunity to shine or fail! Most people who serve in the church are volunteers with other jobs and responsibilities. So, when they don't show up, don't freak out.

Your expectations and their physical abilities may not match. Take care that you don't frustrate, overwhelm, or overwork your volunteers. Remember, they signed up because of their desire to serve.

Help them serve.

They may just need to take another position, or help in another area that doesn't require so much.

Just take care when providing direction, you do so with **their feelings** and needs in mind.

People will offend you.

Leadership calls us to serve beyond offense. Leave your expectations, disappointments and frustrations behind...

"Love suffers long and is kind..."

1 Corinthians 13:4

4 BE STRONG

You will fail. I know, that's not very positive, but it is the truth. Worship leaders will hit **wrong notes**, guitarists may be **off key,** drummers can **miss a beat,** lighting technicians might **miss queues,** sound board operators sometimes hit the **wrong buttons**, ushers occasionally go down the **wrong isles**, and pastors may preach a **boring message or two.** You get the point.

Serving can be like

going to battle.

You must be prepared to fight and sometimes face failure moments.

Don't expect to fail, but don't freak out when you have failure moments.

Faced with impending battle, in the midst of leadership change, Moses told the people,

> Be strong and of good courage, do not fear nor be afraid of them; for the Lord your God, He is the One who goes with you. He will not leave you nor forsake you. (Deuteronomy 31: 6)

The same call to courage was repeated three times in Joshua, "Be strong and courageous." Why did both Moses and Joshua say this to the people? Because when we are faced with great difficulty, **we want to run away and give up.**

Failure has been an unwelcome friend of mine on several occasions. When I was asked to resign from my first pastorate, I was so crushed that I ran off to work in the hills of Pennsylvania for a year. Years later, I tried again, only to resign from my second pastorate because

I let my own cares, desires and worries overwhelm me. Though I've had other **failure moments**, my worst was divorce. All at once, I lost my job, possessions, and family.

Letting those latest failures happen led me to work as a gas station attendant away from my family and alone.

Weakness causes us to run and fail.

We need strength to help us stand in the face of personal, emotional and spiritual trouble. I could have remained physically and emotionally separated from people, **but I finally came to my senses.**

My first step to regained strength was to come to a humble realization of my failures. It is best to realize and face one's own failings than to try to run from them. **They will catch up to you anyway.**

My next step was to **act upon my realization.** There is an often quoted truth,

"Don't be sorry, be different."

It is **useless** to wallow in regret, hide from our mistakes and run from our battles of ministry and service.

What that meant for me, was that I had to **move back** to the town where many knew of my failures. It also meant **finding new ways to minister and serve** for the good of God's kingdom.

Finally, **I surrendered** to God's Word and Spirit to change me. **I prayed** to God for help, **read** and **listened** to His Holy Word, and **joined a fellowship** of Christians who would **hold me accountable** to change.

If you want to be in ministry you must realize that we are in spiritual warfare and the battles are hard.

Search the Word, and your heart.

Seek fellowship to help

keep you strong

5 BE FLEXIBLE

There is an old proverb, "The flexible shall not be broken."

You have great ideas and plans. **Are you ready to throw them all out**? If not, then you are not ready to serve in ministry.

While we should seek to serve in areas that lie within our passions, it is more important to serve where we are needed, then where we want.

Change will come.

Positions, styles, church needs, and the needs of the people will change. It is crucial to recognize that there are seasons of ministry. Just because you are working in one area now, does not mean you won't be working in another area later.

When I was a teenager, I led worship for my youth group. Then, when I went to Bible School, I became one of the school's worship leaders. After that, I served as a worship leader for two churches and numerous Christian retreats.

Musical styles and preferences have changed over the years.

My voice is not what it used to be. For a number of reasons, my season as a head worship leader is over. Just like my season of being a pastor is over.

In both instances, it was difficult to come to the realization that it was time to move on and let go of the past. **But it was necessary.**

We must always **seek** to match our present abilities with the current needs, while being **ready and willing to move** and flow with the changes as they come.

It is also important to know that everyone is replaceable. Don't think you are any different. No matter how much you are doing, or how many people depend upon your work, when you leave, **someone will be there to fill the gap.**

It's even possible that your

replacement will be

better than you.

I can honestly say that it is a great joy for me to see my former churches **have progressed to greater levels of worship and ministry.**

It is easy to think of favorite areas of ministry as our children. But, at some point, our babies will no longer belong to us.

We have to let them grow up and leave our nests.

To serve effectively is to give people what they need, not what you want to give. Going to church is not about getting what you can out of the music, or the sermon.

It is about being part of a community, where we serve each other and help each other grow into strong, victorious Christian men and women.

Listen to the words of Peter, as he speaks in 1 Peter 2: 1- 5

> Therefore, **laying aside** all malice, all deceit, hypocrisy, envy, and all evil speaking, as newborn babes, **desire** the pure milk of the Word that you may grow thereby, if indeed you have tasted that the Lord is gracious. Coming to Him as to a living stone, rejected indeed by men, but chosen by God and precious, you also, as living stones, **are being built up** a spiritual house, a holy priesthood, to offer up **spiritual sacrifices** acceptable to God through Jesus Christ.

We have to grow emotionally and spiritually before we can help others grow. Growing requires **flexibility** through change, **even when the change hurts.**

6 BE PREPARED

I hate to admit there have been times when I have led worship without knowing the music. I have preached sermons for which I have not prepared and taught classes for which I did not study. In all cases, the outcome **has not been pleasant**.

I have forgotten words, stammered over sermon points, and stood in silence in front of congregations while searching my thoughts.

It is embarrassing
to be unprepared.
Not only that,
it is uncomfortable
for your audience.

At one company where I worked, I had an opportunity to move into a better area. To get the position I wanted, I had to use my lunch time, come early and stay late, with no extra pay, to learn how to do it.

When the opportunity arose, I was the only person in the company prepared to take the position. So, I was awarded a promotion and more money.

The same principle is true in church ministry. If you want to be successful, you have to spend time preparing for the work.

Preparation will bring rewards.

The apostle Paul said in 2 Timothy 2: 15,

"Be diligent to present yourself approved to God, a worker who does not need to be ashamed, rightly dividing the word of truth."

Paul also says in 2 Timothy 4:2 to "...be ready in season and out of season." You need to be ready to speak, sing, counsel, teach, or serve and be ready to do it with correctly.

Reading scriptures **in advance**, helps the Holy Spirit bring them to mind when needed. Getting the words to songs **in your heart** will help you get your eyes off the paper and on the people.

Practice, study, arrive early, and stay late. Do what it takes to learn and serve effectively. Spend time in worship and the Word **before** you arrive. When you start with your heart, you'll be **ready to serve** the people around you. Once you are at church, you don't have time to get ready.

You're on!

Finally, in Colossians 3:23, we read "...whatever you do, do it heartily, as to the Lord and not to men."

Be prepared to do what God needs you to do!

7 BE REAL

This be-attitude is followed by a couple of don'ts. **Don't** over commit and **don't** try to be something you're not.

Being real means

knowing your limitations.

For instance, if you know you can't sing, **please don't try to join the praise team.** If you can't play, **don't try to be in the band**. If you put yourself to sleep when you teach, **don't try to lead a Bible study**.

If your family has something going on every night of the week except for one, it might **not** be a good idea to try to lead a group on that one night.

Another consideration is public failure. Don't be afraid to fail in front of those you are serving, or to talk about past or present failures, as in Chapter 4.

It is from our failures and the failures of others that we best learn and grow.

Another thing is that if you try to hide your faults, or your past, **people will find out**.

Then, you will look like a hypocrite and a fool. We don't need any more of those!

Besides serving in spite of our failures and weaknesses, it is important to know when to say "No."

While there is always a need for more volunteers, especially faithful ones, it is also important that you don't overdo and work to the point of exhaustion.

Count the cost of service.

Jesus said,

> For which of you, intending to build a tower, does not sit down first and count the cost, whether he has enough to finish it— lest, after he has laid the foundation, and is not able to finish, all who see it begin to mock him, saying, 'This man began to build and was not able to finish.' Or what king, going to make war against another king, does not sit down first and consider whether he is able with ten thousand to meet him who comes against him with twenty thousand? Or else, while the other is still a great way off, he sends a delegation and asks conditions of peace. Luke 14: 28-32

Nearly every church needs more help. Too many people sit and receive, while needs go unmet. But, before you jump in to help, make sure you are either ready, or are willing to do what it takes to get ready.

Before you sign up, make sure you are willing and able to show up and fill in as needed.

8 BE LOVING

All Christians are called to love, compassion, empathy, and to have a servant's heart. Those callings are amplified for those in any form of ministry. When people say, "I want to be in ministry," they usually really mean they want to be the **head honcho** and get paid enough to pay all their bills. But what many don't realize is that it takes many people to keep a church running.

Let me rephrase that, it takes a lot of people to keep a **healthy** church running. Not only that, but **it is impossible to pay everyone that serves in a church.** Some are better off to be left unpaid anyhow.

Moving from volunteer to paid ministry puts a different dynamic on one's relationship with the pastor, people and the work. Being paid can make ministry look **more like work** than service to God. But, paid and unpaid ministers are equal in their importance in the body of Christ and in a **healthy church**.

I've been that pastor that opened and locked up for every service. I turned on the heat, lights, sound, and set up and turned it all off again when I was done.

I printed the bulletins and newsletters, mailed them out, visited the homebound and hospitalized, and preached all the sermons. My church didn't grow much because I didn't let it.

Doing it all yourself is not love.

It is micro management.

In healthy churches, leaders **hire and delegate** paid staff and volunteers. In addition, a few do not hold all the power, nor do all the work. People interact, cross train in ministries and serve when and where called upon.

Something else to think about is how we feel about those we serve. While love compels us to do more that we are expected, hate, fear and contempt make service a living hell.

If the people we serve get on our last nerve, it is time for an attitude adjustment.

Or, it is time to move on!

1 Corinthians 13: 1-3 teaches about love this way...

> Though I speak with the tongues of men and of angels, but have not love, **I have become sounding brass or a clanging cymbal**. And though I have the gift of prophecy, and understand all mysteries and all knowledge, and though I have all faith, so that I could remove mountains, but have not love, **I am nothing**. And though I bestow all my goods to feed the poor, and though I give my body to be burned, but have not love, **it profits me nothing.**

To be effective in ministry, one must serve according to the need.

If someone needs you to listen,

don't counsel.

Just because you are called upon to visit someone in the hospital, **does not mean you are now the church chaplain. They may never need you to do it again.**

If the church needs an usher, or media person more than they need a praise team member, it may be better for you to **do what is needed** until someone else steps up so you can do what you really want.

You do well to consider serving in your church. I only say that you should keep the be-attitudes in mind and make sure you are ready.

In honor of Jeff Foxworthy's famous bit, "You might be a redneck if...," I conclude with some attitudes that one **should not** have if going to serve in ministry.

If you like being served more than serving, you might not be ready to serve.

If you can't take criticism, or offend easily, you might not be ready to serve.

If you run from trouble instead of facing it head on, you might not be ready to serve.

If you are not flexible and can't tolerate change, you might not be ready to serve.

If you are unwilling to learn, practice, or prepare, you might not be ready to serve.

If you cannot say no, or are unwilling to bare your faults and fail in front of others, you might not be ready to serve.

Most importantly, **if you can't stand people and are serving more out of a sense of obligation than heartfelt desire,** you might not be ready to serve.

So, are you still ready to serve?

Then please go ahead!

We need you.

But we need you to be: a servant, patient, strong, flexible, prepared, real, and loving…

Go forth and serve.

I conclude with the words of Jesus from Matthew 28:18-20

> All authority has been given to Me in heaven and on earth. **Go** therefore and make disciples of all the nations, baptizing them in the name of the Father and of the Son and of the Holy Spirit, teaching them to observe all things that I have commanded you; and lo, I am with you always, even to the end of the age.

OTHER RESOURCE

Here are a few other resources about church leadership.

"So, you're thinking of being a pastor?"

Author: Joe Thorn,

http://www.joethorn.net/2007/05/08/so-youre-thinking-of-being-a-pastor/

Understanding God's Call: A Ministry Inquiry Process, Author: Sharon G. Rubey, Publisher: Board of Higher Education and Ministry, 2009

Called to Lead: 26 Leadership Lessons from the Life of the Apostle Paul,

Author: John MacArthur, Publisher: Thomas Nelson, 2010)

Post Traumatic Church Disorder,

Author: Jason E Roberts, Publisher: CreateSpace Independent Publishing Platform, 2012

ACKNOWLEDGMENTS

I give thanks to God, and those who have helped me learn how to serve God with humility, passion, intensity, and flexibility. These include, but are not limited to Pastor Derek Capello of Northridge Church, my mom, Margaret Johnson, my wife, Stephanie, Pastors Terry Exley, Josh Brewer, Randy Brown, Tom Binford, Lynn Hill, Paul Colossi, and T. Thornton. I also thank Mike Parsons, who gave me feedback and encouragement while writing this book.

ABOUT THE AUTHOR

Don Terry has failed. It's important that we start there. You don't care to hear him brag about all his great accomplishments anyway. You just want to hear the nitty gritty good stuff.

Fair enough. Don has learned more from failing than from success. So, all of the words of encouragement and exhortation are born from his failures. This book is more of a do as he says, not as he did sort of thing. He has been proud, arrogant, impatient, unloving, weak, hateful and unqualified.

Don Terry now works as a Purchasing Associate in Brentwood, TN and lives in a small town called White House , TN with his wife and two boys. He sings as part of a praise team, and teaches Bible studies at The Northridge Church, writes and records music, and blogs at iSing4God.com.

He would love to hear what you thought about the book. Or, if you like to hang out with people who have failed, but serve anyway, feel free to contact him at:

Email: donterry@ising4God.com

Blog: www.iSing4God.com

Twitter: @DonTerry_

Facebook: (Look up iSing4God.com)

LinkedIn: http://www.linkedin.com/in/dlterry

www.ingramcontent.com/pod-product-compliance
Lightning Source LLC
LaVergne TN
LVHW020313110826
845148LV00017BA/2669

* 9 7 8 0 6 1 5 6 9 3 9 1 0 *